UNITED STATES CIVICS
THE US CONSTITUTION FOR KIDS

**1787 – 2016 WITH AMENDMENTS
4TH GRADE SOCIAL STUDIES**

In this book, we're going to talk
about the United States Constitution.
So, let's get right to it!

WHAT IS THE CONSTITUTION?

The Constitution is the basis for all the laws that are passed in the United States. It lays out a plan for how the democratic government of the US should work. The government is separated into three different parts called branches.

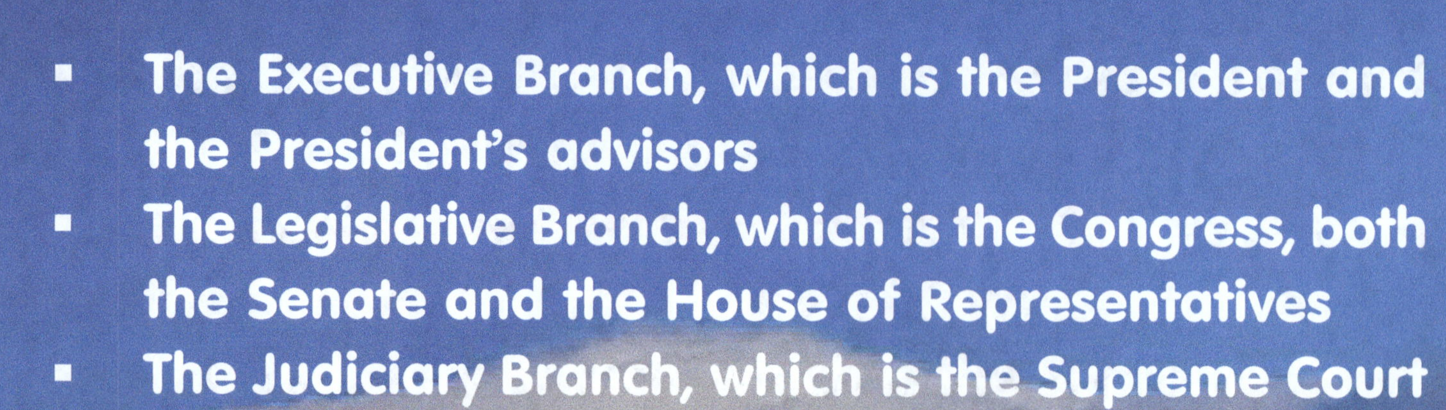

The Executive Branch, which is the President and the President's advisors
The Legislative Branch, which is the Congress, both the Senate and the House of Representatives
The Judiciary Branch, which is the Supreme Court

THE WHITE HOUSE

Every state has a constitution as well. Just as the United States Constitution is the most important law of the land, the state constitutions carry their most important laws as well. However the US Constitution is more important since it is federal law.

SUPREME COURT

We the People

insure domestic Tranquility, provide for th[e]
and our Posterity, do ordain and establish

Powers here[in]

Section. 1. All legislative Powers
of Representatives.

Section. 2. The House of Representatives
in each State shall have the Qualifications requi[site]
No Person shall be a Representative who shall not, when elected, be an Inhab[itant]
Representatives and direct Taxes sha[ll]
be determined by ad[ding]
Persons

The Constitution can be altered if necessary. When the Constitution is changed, it is "amended" and an amendment is added to its document. At the current time, there have been 27 of these amendments that have been added. It is extremely difficult to get a new amendment passed so there have been many amendments that were proposed but never passed.

Many of the amendments that were approved are about the rights of individuals. The first group of ten amendments has a special name. It is described as the "Bill of Rights."

ll of Rights
ress OF THE United States,
Begun and held at the City of New York, on
the fourth of March, one thousand seven hundred and eighty nine.

HISTORY OF THE UNITED STATES CONSTITUTION

The United States won its independence from Great Britain in 1783. From May of 1787 to September of that same year, a group of representatives convened to begin the important task of creating the Constitution for the new country.

This group described themselves as the "Framers" since they were going to frame or outline the initial laws for the United States. The government wasn't working smoothly yet so their goal was to put things in writing so that it would provide guidelines for the checks and balances in the government. Some of the members of this group are well known names from history, such as George Washington and Benjamin Franklin.

GEORGE WASHINGTON

At this time in United States history there weren't the fifty states that there are today. There were only thirteen. Representatives from these thirteen came to the Convention, except for the state of Rhode Island. Of course, it was difficult for the men to agree on what should be included in the Constitution so they talked and debated for endless hours over the hot summer months in Philadelphia.

THE RHODE ISLAND STATE HOUSE

BENJAMIN FRANKLIN

They had to agree and compromise in order to come up with a plan that was workable. Benjamin Franklin at one point declared that even though the plan wasn't perfect it was as perfect as a piece of legislature could get.

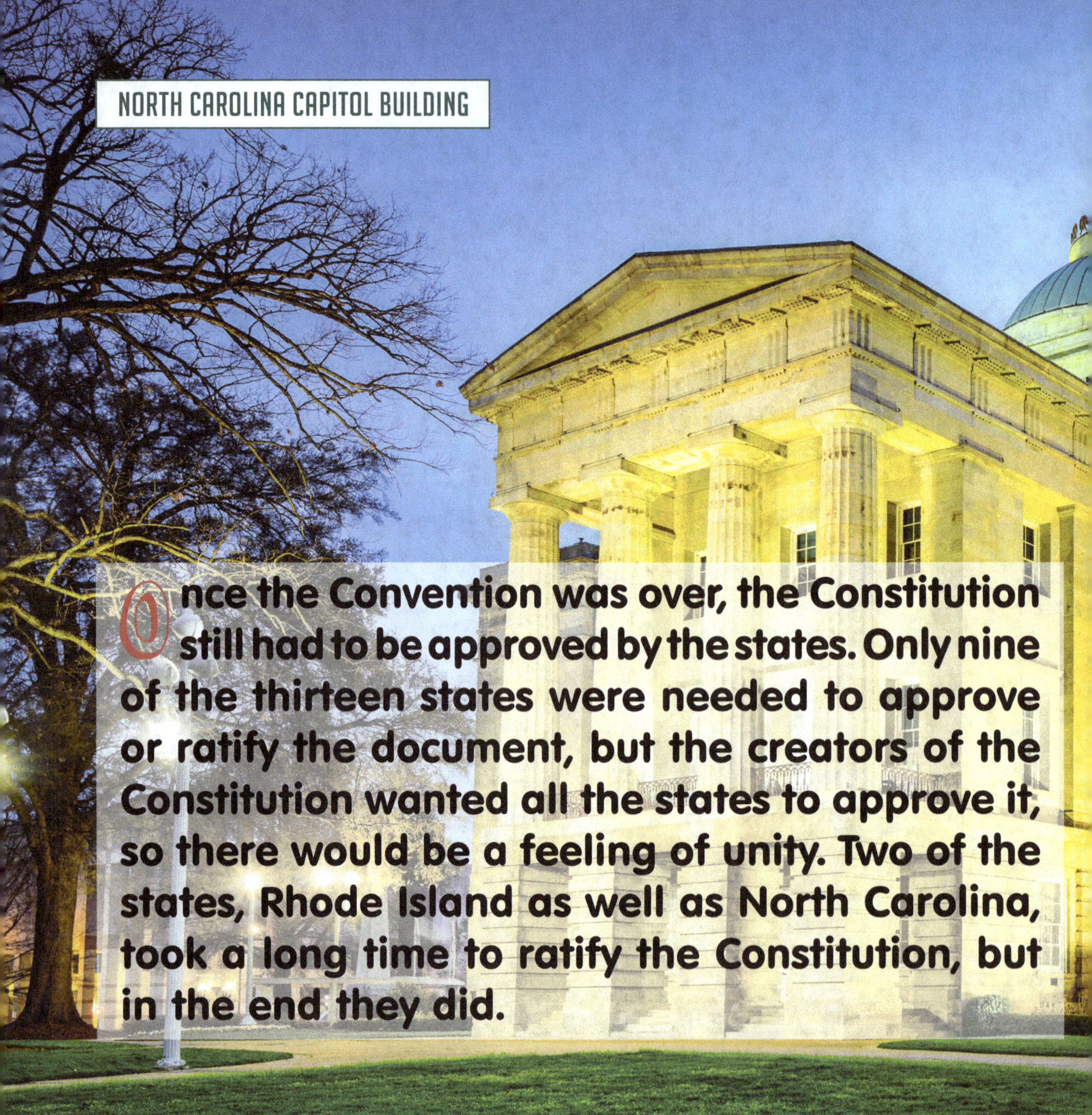

Once the Convention was over, the Constitution still had to be approved by the states. Only nine of the thirteen states were needed to approve or ratify the document, but the creators of the Constitution wanted all the states to approve it, so there would be a feeling of unity. Two of the states, Rhode Island as well as North Carolina, took a long time to ratify the Constitution, but in the end they did.

THE AMENDMENT PROCESS

The Framers realized that their document wasn't ideal. They knew that future representatives would have good suggestions to add to the Constitution. They decided to create a process for amending the Constitution. They wanted to make sure that the process of making a change wasn't too simple.

fter all, the Constitution was the basis for the entire running of the government so it shouldn't be too easy to make changes to it. On the other hand, it shouldn't be impossible to amend the Constitution either. As time went on, changes would occur that would make it necessary to add other amendments to the Constitution.

ution

Constitu

One of the reasons that some states were reluctant to ratify the original Constitution was because it didn't specify a list of rights that citizens should have that the government should never violate. The right to be free to speak your own mind or the right to worship in the way you see fit are two rights that are examples of individual rights.

onal rights

Some of the original Framers didn't think this "bill of rights" was necessary, but others pushed for it, so in 1791 an additional 10 amendments regarding individual freedoms were added to the Constitution. They were officially called the "Bill of Rights."

BILL OF
IGHTS

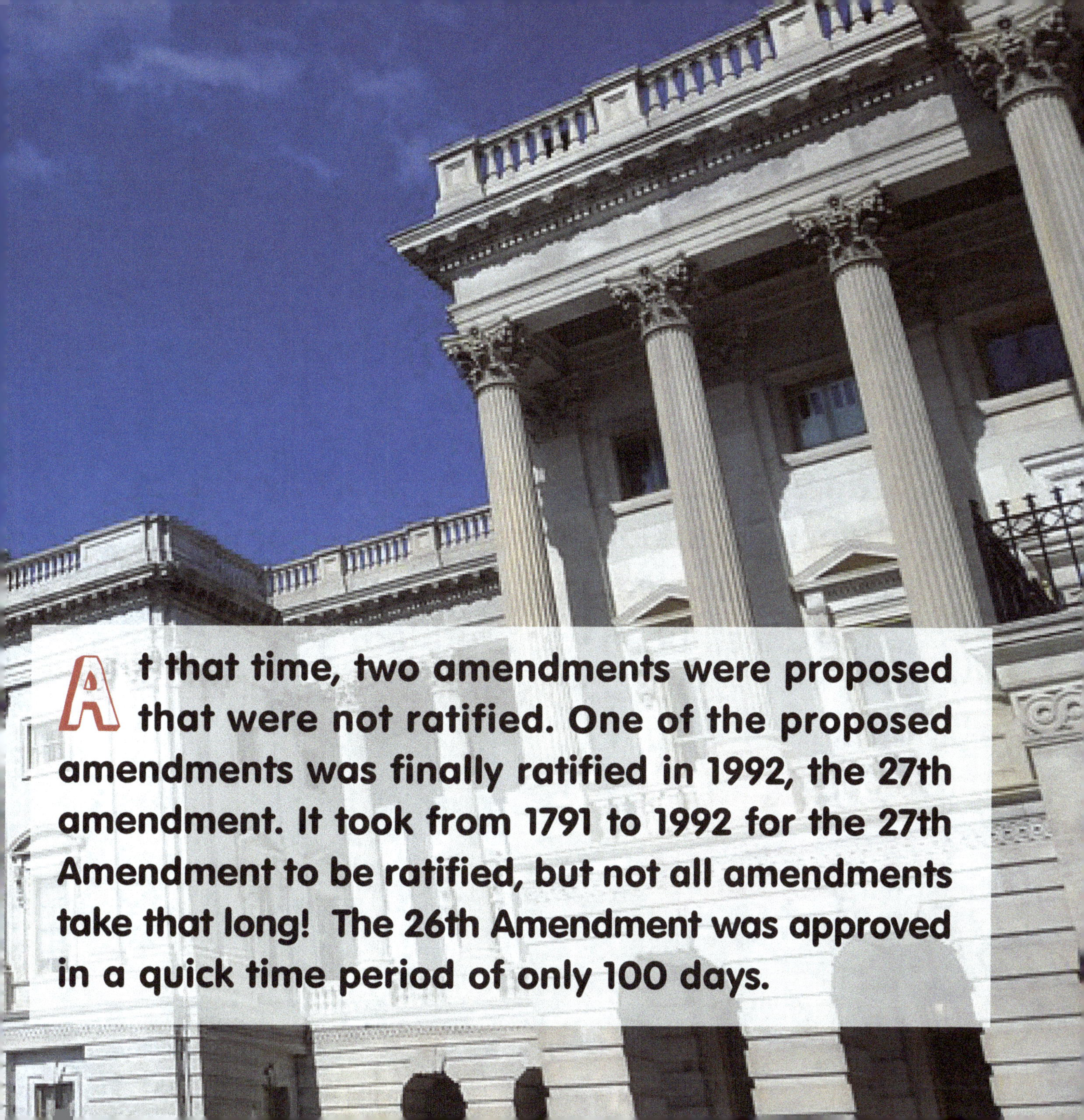

At that time, two amendments were proposed that were not ratified. One of the proposed amendments was finally ratified in 1992, the 27th amendment. It took from 1791 to 1992 for the 27th Amendment to be ratified, but not all amendments take that long! The 26th Amendment was approved in a quick time period of only 100 days.

THE BILL OF RIGHTS

James Madison drafted the document that would eventually become the Bill of Rights. Ten of the twelve amendments he proposed to the Constitution were ratified. They protect the freedoms of individual citizens.

JAMES MADISION

FIRST AMENDMENT, which guarantees that an individual can speak freely and worship the way he or she wants to

SECOND AMENDMENT, which guarantees that an individual can own a firearm for protection

THIRD AMENDMENT, which guarantees that the government cannot house soldiers in your home

FOURTH AMENDMENT, which guarantees that the government cannot conduct a search inside your home without a warrant

FIFTH AMENDMENT, which guarantees that you don't have to testify against yourself in court

SIXTH AMENDMENT, which guarantees a relatively quick trial in court by a jury of citizens who are not prejudiced against your case

COURTROOM

SEVENTH AMENDMENT, which guarantees that civil court cases be tried by juries

EIGHTH AMENDMENT, which guarantees that citizens won't be given unusual punishments that are cruel

NINTH AMENDMENT, which states that citizens have other rights that are not stated specifically in the Constitution

TENTH AMENDMENT, which states that if the United States government isn't specifically listed has having a particular power, then the state governments or the people have it

SLAVES

THE ISSUE OF SLAVERY

When the Constitution was being drafted in 1787, many of the black people living in the United States were slaves. They worked in the homes and businesses of white people. Many people didn't feel that it was right in a free country that some people didn't have freedom.

They began to speak openly about ending slavery. These individuals were described as abolitionists. There was a geographic separation between those people who wanted to end slavery and those who didn't. In most cases, the people in the Northern states wanted slavery to be a thing of the past, while those in the Southern states wanted to keep slavery.

The South depended on slavery for their economy. Most of their profits came from plantations that grew cotton or tobacco and slaves were needed to do the hard labor.

ABRAHAM LINCOLN

When President Abraham Lincoln was elected to office, tensions came to a head. States from the South left the United States to form their own country, the Confederate States. The United States government didn't want these states to leave the country and the Civil War was fought, North against South from the years 1861 to 1865.

It was a very bloody war and many lives were lost, but the North was victorious. The United States was united once more. Slavery was abolished and an Amendment was added to the Constitution.

The next three amendments were important to the freedoms of all Americans:

THE 13TH AMENDMENT

This amendment abolished slavery in the United States. It made it a federal offense to keep slaves.

THE 14TH AMENDMENT

This amendment stated that every person who was born on United States land was a United States citizen with full rights. This included people who had been slaves before.

THE 15TH AMENDMENT

This amendment gave African American males the ability and the right to cast their vote in elections.

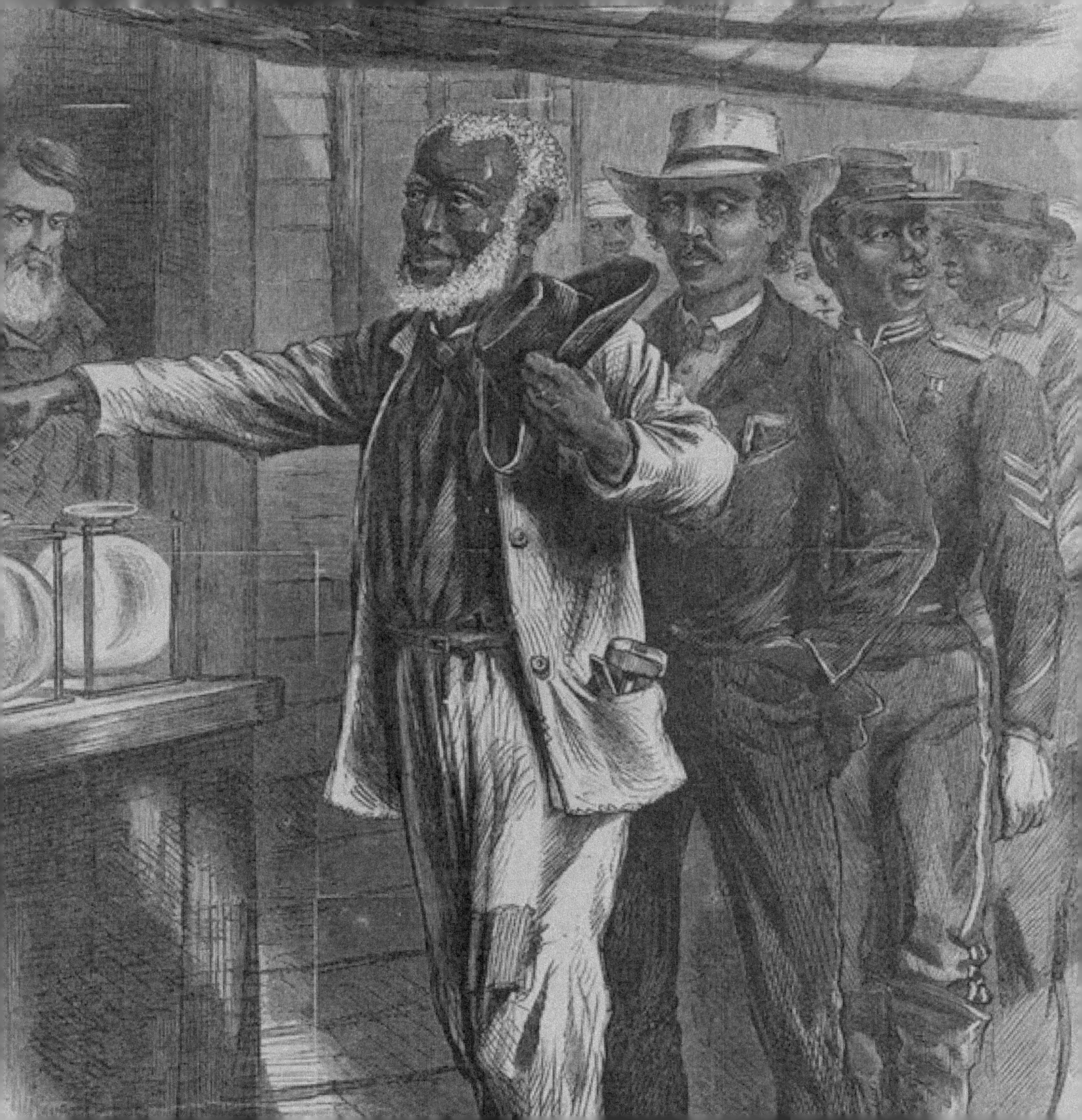

BARACK OBAMA

espite these laws, it took a long time for the attitude toward African Americans to change in the South. Today, there are still some people who harbor racial prejudice, but most people in the United States agree that everyone should have equal rights no matter what color their skin is. In 2009, Barack Obama was the first African-American to become President. He was the 44th President and served two terms.

WOMEN'S RIGHTS

For many years, men were the only ones who had powerful roles in the United States government, but this isn't true any longer. Beginning in the late 1800s, women and men spoke out about the fact that women weren't allowed to vote or take part in the government. It took over 70 years, but thanks to brave women such as Elizabeth Cady Stanton and her colleague Susan B. Anthony, women were eventually given the right to vote.

ELIZABETH CADY STANTON AND SUSAN B. ANTHONY

In the year 1920, the 19th Amendment was ratified giving women the right to vote. Today there are many women who play important roles in the United States government.

THE US CONSTITUTION

The Constitution of the United States created three branches of government and the way that each of those three would regulate the others to keep the power in balance. Those three branches are the Legislative, which is Congress, the Executive, which is the President and the President's advisors, and the judiciary, which is the Supreme Court. The 27 Amendments to the Constitution deal largely with the rights of individuals and these include the first 10 Amendments, which are described as the Bill of Rights. The Bill of Rights protects important individual freedoms, such as freedom of speech and freedom to practice your own religion.

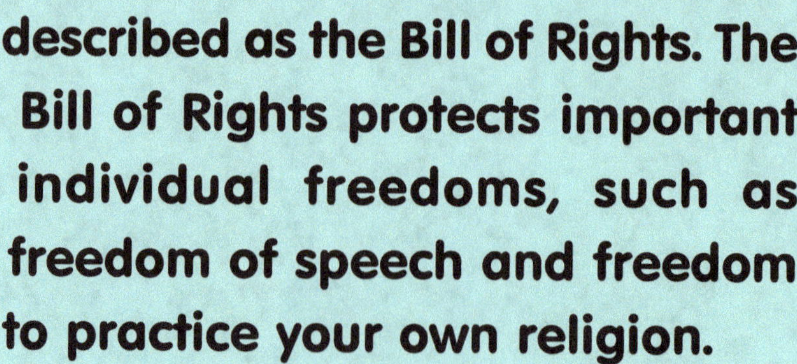

CAPITAL BUILDING, WASHINGTON DC

Awesome! Now that you've read about the United States Constitution, you may want to read more about the United States Cabinet in the Baby Professor book *The US Cabinet: The President's Top Advisors.*

Visit

BABY PROFESSOR
EDUCATION KIDS

www.BabyProfessorBooks.com
to download Free Baby Professor eBooks
and view our catalog of new and exciting
Children's Books